Life's Little Construction Book

Willoughby Books, Inc. • Austin, Texas
By Rick Villani & Chuck Faust

Anyone who has spent the greater part of a day completing a project that should have taken 15 or 20 minutes will benefit from the time-saving wisdom and common-sense advice in Life's Little Construction Book.

-Rick Villani & Chuck Faust, Authors

If you have a handy tip of your
own and would like to
submit it for our next edition of
Life's Little Construction Book
or would simply like to write us
with your comments, please do so at

Willoughby Books, Inc.

P.O. Box 9491 • Austin, Texas 78766-9491

Dedicated to...

Carrie, Emily, and Jack
Elizabeth and Leslie

Special thanks to...

Susan Villani for layout, Jolly Design for cover,
Paige Hamilton for editing, and special
thanks to Veronica Coronado.

If it ain't broke, don't fix it.

To test the squareness of a project, measure diagonally from point to point. If the measurements are equal it is square.

Buy hammers with steel-forged heads. They are stronger.

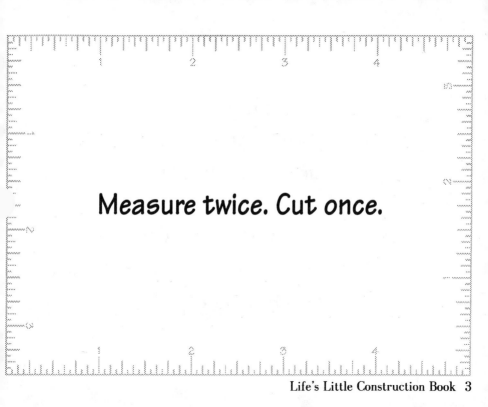

Measure twice. Cut once.

To find a leak in a pipe or a tire, brush on soapy water. A bubble will form over the leak .

When the temperature dips below 32 degrees, let your faucets drip to help keep pipes from freezing.

A 2 x 4 is not really two inches by
four inches. It is usually
1 1/2 inches by 3 1/2 inches.

To sand hard-to-reach areas on
chair legs or rungs, cut sandpaper
into thin strips.

To make a simple depth gauge,
attach a piece of masking
tape to your drill bit.

To prevent splintering while
drilling, clamp a piece of scrap wood
underneath the piece you are drilling.

When painting a
smooth surface, plan to use one
gallon of paint for every
450 square feet.

To calculate square footage,
multiply length times width.

When doing plumbing work, protect finished faucets and surfaces by covering the ends of your tools with electrical tape.

Pre-milled lumber is always measured thickness first and width second.

When cutting into a wall, make
sure there are no wires or pipes
behind your cutting area.

When hammering, angle nails
slightly toward each other to
provide more holding power.

When mounting a cleat for
a shelf, angle nails downward to
provide more stability.

To thaw frozen pipes use a hand-
held dryer. Keep the dryer moving
from the faucet back to the wall.

When mitering wood for a project, cut the mitered end first, then re-measure and cut the straight end. That way, if you make a mistake while mitering you get a second chance with the same piece of wood.

The most durable caulking
compounds have a latex base.

To prevent air bubbles when
varnishing or lacquering, wipe the
brush on the inside of the
can instead of the rim.

Use a voltage tester to make sure
an outlet is safe to work on.

If you don't have a voltage tester,
plug a lamp or radio into
the outlet to test whether or
not the power is on.

When planning a project, allow
10% extra material for wastage.

When taping and floating drywall,
use self-adhesive fiberglass mesh
tape instead of paper tape.
It's faster and easier to use.

Don't clean paint rollers during short breaks. Instead, wrap them in plastic bags.

White or off-white paint is less expensive and saves energy due to light-reflecting power.

As a general rule, don't make improvements that will raise the value of your house more than 30%. You may price yourself out of the market.

Don't settle for vague estimates from contractors.

A rented screw or nail
gun is worth its cost on a large
project due to saved time and
increased efficiency.

Rent tools that you will
probably use only once.

A fresh coat of paint can return
ten times the investment when
selling your house.

After a coat of paint,
wallpaper is the most affordable
new finish for a wall.

The most economical
way to refurbish drywall is to
patch and paint.

Strain old paint
through a screen or panty hose
to remove lumps.

Fluorescent lights provide more
light and are less expensive to
operate than incandescent lights.

Too much insulation will
cost more than it will ever save in
reduced fuel costs.

When pulling nails, add extra leverage by putting a block of wood under the head of the hammer or pry bar.

Wear rubber gloves when working with solvents.

Draw reference marks
on your circular saw to make
it easier to guide.

Fix what is fixable, replace
what can't be fixed, and add only
what is necessary.

To prevent rust on your table saw,
apply paste wax to the table.
Wood will also slide across the
table more easily.

Use C-clamps as handles to
carry sheets of plywood.

For precise measuring
with a tape measure, start
from the 1" mark. It is
more accurate because
the tape's end hook usually
has some play in it.

Prolong the shelf life of latex paint by breathing into the can before sealing.

Foam gaskets placed inside outlets and switches save energy.

To paint the bottom of a door
without removing it, slide an old
piece of carpet coated with paint
underneath the door.

Use pressure treated lumber to
reduce the chances of termites.

Attach pegboard to the side
legs of your workbench for extra
storage space.

To make screws and nails go into
wood more easily, rub them with
bees wax or a bar of soap.

When taking apart a project put double-sided tape on your workbench and arrange the pieces on the tape in their proper order.

Spray furniture wax on your shovel to keep snow from sticking to it.

Burn the end
of a nylon rope to keep it
from unraveling.

Coat the end of a hemp
rope with shellac to keep it
from unraveling.

Use vegetable oil to
clean your hands after using
an oil-based paint.

When using a plunger, close
the overflow holes in your sink or
tub to increase suction.

When hanging a door,
line up the hinges by standing
the door on a towel or small
stack of newspapers.

Vinegar can be used to loosen
old glue joints.

Put excess sawdust in your
compost pile.

To prevent pliers from scratching
a project, cut off the fingers of
an old pair of gloves and slip them
over the jaws of the pliers.

To put a screw in a hard-to-reach
place, push it through the
sticky side of a piece of
masking tape and then wrap
the tape around the shaft
of the screwdriver.

Lining your tool drawer with an old
piece of carpet can keep tools from
shifting around.

Paint inch and foot markers
on your workshop floor to quickly
measure lumber.

Separate nails, screws, nuts, and bolts
in old baby food jars. Then screw or nail
the lids to the underside of a shelf.

Spray soapy water on gas lines to
help spot gas leaks. Bubbles should
appear where there is a leak.

Label your circuit
breakers to prevent repeated
trial and error.

When labeling your circuit breakers, plug a loud radio into various outlets to discover which circuit each outlet occupies.

Put petroleum jelly around the ring of a plunger to increase suction.

To remove a broken-off
light bulb, turn the power
off at the circuit breaker
and then jam a potato or
bar of soap into the bulb
and twist it out.

Ground a metal work bench to
a cold-water pipe.

Flashlights are easier to find
in the dark if the handles
are painted with luminous paint or
encircled with luminous tape.

Stab loose drill bits and
nail punches into a foam block
attached to your workbench.

Store sandpaper and abrasive
sheets in plastic bags to
prolong their life.

Be conservative when calculating
how long a project will take.
Add up how long you think it will
take, and then double it.

Chalk on the tip of a screwdriver will
help remove a slippery screw.

Spray silicone on your drill bits
before each use to make them
last longer.

Keep a file box in your workshop
to store manuals and
warranties for your tools.

Spray-paint small objects
inside a cardboard box to contain
stray paint drops.

To tighten a loose wooden
handle, soak it in linseed oil.
It should make the wood swell.

Nail a yardstick to the front of your workbench for easy measuring.

To determine the proper penny equivalent for nails, subtract a half-inch from the length of the nail you need, then multiply by four.

Strap nails to the handle of your hammer with a rubber band so they will be easily accessible.

Rub chalk in the indentations of a metal framing square to make it easier to read.

If the head of a screw is stripped,
angle the point of a center-punch
against the screw head and
hit it with a hammer.

Roll putty over the teeth of a file
to clean out small particles.

Store plywood upright as
it is more prone to warping when
stored flat.

A piece of measuring tape glued
down the handle of your hammer
will prove to be convenient.

To measure how full a propane tank is, make a wet streak down its side. The moisture will evaporate from the empty portion first.

Use a magnet to remove small pieces of steel wool from a project.

For a handy reference
while at the store, keep a three
inch section of tape measure
in your wallet.

Use cotton swabs to do
touch-up painting.

When you are finished spray painting, turn the can upside down and spray until the nozzle is clear to prevent clogging.

When painting, a light color makes a room look larger.

Push a broom handle through
the hollow rung of an extension
ladder to hang paint cans
from the handles.

Stand a paint roller on end after
cleaning to prevent it from matting.

Use a nail to punch holes in the rim of a paint can to allow excess paint to drip back into the can.

To cut down on drips while painting, do not dip your brush more than halfway up the bristles.

To prevent rust in gutter downspouts, paint the inside by attaching a string to a sponge and pulling it through the down spout.

To soften stiff paintbrush bristles soak them in vinegar.

For more strength, attach
plywood sheets with their grain
running perpendicular to wall studs.

If you lose your glue cap,
use a screw-on wire nut as a
replacement.

To hide a finishing nail, use a
nail set to drive the head
below the surface, and then cover
the hole with wood putty.

Always drill a pilot hole before
using a lag screw.

To find a wall stud without
special tools, tap the wall with
your knuckles. A hollow sound is
a space; a solid sound is a stud.

To remove rust from a nut, drop it
into a glass of cola.

Wire mesh on your gutters will act
as a leaf guard and still allow
water to run through.

Slide cotton socks over the top
ends of your extension ladder to
prevent marking the wall.

After sawing metal, use a magnet wrapped in plastic wrap to clean off small pieces of metal. Then pull the plastic off over a trash can.

Rubber bands can be used as clamps when gluing small objects.

If you blow a fuse on an essential circuit, you can temporarily replace it with a less important fuse of the same amperage until you can replace the blown fuse.

When working with electricity, try not to come in contact with plumbing pipes as the pipes may have been used as grounds.

A good deal of clogged plumbing can be fixed with a plunger.

Do not use a plastic pipe to replace
a metal pipe in a line that may have
been used as a ground.

Cover water pipes with
insulation jackets to prevent
condensation or freezing.

To remove a **stubborn** nut,
try applying a lubricant, a soft
drink, peroxide, ammonia, or a light
oil. If none of these work, try
heating the nut with a hand-held
dryer and then letting it cool.

To help remove a rusty nut,
rub it with a steel brush.
If nothing else works, try cutting
it off with a hacksaw blade.

Always remove masking tape
before the paint completely dries.

If you smell gas, get
everyone out of the house
immediately. Use a friend's
phone to call the gas company.

Wear thick gloves when working with
rough or jagged edges.

Ventilate your attic to conserve energy.

Insulate your water heater to
conserve energy and save money.

Keep all of your blades sharp to
make cutting faster and easier.

Keep a first aid kit in plain sight.

Keep electrical cords away from cutting edges.

Keep a fire extinguisher in your workshop.

Keep children and pets away from
your work area.

Be sure all of your cords and
outlets are properly grounded.

Never overload an electrical outlet.

Always use safety
glasses or goggles.

Check your flashlights
regularly to make sure the
batteries are fresh.

Before starting a project,
test your tools to make sure they
are in proper working order.

Work where
you can be heard if you
become injured.

A good workbench
is key to a good
workshop.

When cutting wood
with the grain
use a rip saw.

When cutting wood
against the grain
use a cross-cut saw.

A Phillips-head screwdriver
has a tip shaped like a
plus (+) sign.

A flat head screwdriver
has a tip shaped like a
minus (-) sign.

Use retractable utility knives
instead of non-retractable knives.
They are safer.

To extend the life of a
wooden ladder, varnish it to prevent
it from drying out.

A linear foot is
measured in terms of the
length of the board.

A board foot is
measured in terms of the
width of the board.

Vertical levelness is called "plumb".

Horizontal levelness is called "level".

Tie back loose hair and clothing
and remove jewelry before operating
tools or machinery.

Plywood usually comes in
4 foot by 8 foot sheets and in
thicknesses of 1/4 inch, 1/2 inch,
5/8 inch, 3/4 inch and 1 inch.

Use masonry bits for drilling in
concrete, brick, or plaster.

Use an old garden hose as a sheath for
the teeth of a hand saw or hack saw.

To remove a pane of cracked glass
and minimize stray shards,
affix tape to both sides, then
tap the glass out.

A good way to check for
gutter problems is to look at the
ground under the gutters.
If you find depressions, they
were probably formed by leaks
in the gutters above.

To prevent soil erosion at the
bottom of a gutter downspout
add a three foot extension
to the end of the downspout.
Drill holes at 3 to 6 inch
intervals to disperse the water.

Save time when taking off old
shingles. Instead of throwing them on
the ground, put them in trash bags
and then lower them to the ground.

Attach window boxes with
pin hinges for easy removal.

You will save the most energy
and money by having the
recommended amount of insulation
installed in your attic.

Mark where you are going to cut
on the side that will not show.

Instead of using a funnel to put oil in your chain-saw, use a small-tipped squeeze bottle.

If your chain-saw is leaving sawdust rather than chips, it is time to sharpen it.

When your blade hits a
knot while sawing, feed the blade
slowly and let the blade
do the cutting. Do not force it.

Use a vise to secure hard-to-clamp
objects for drilling.

Apply caulking around a sink or tub while it is filled with water. The weight of the water will open the seams more and will allow for a better seal.

Lubricate the locks around your house with graphite twice a year.

To drill at a perpendicular angle, stand a combination square next to the drill, and keep the drill parallel to the square while drilling.

Most wall studs are 16 inches apart, however, some are 24 inches apart.

When drilling iron or steel, use a
light oil to lubricate the bit.
It will make the cut easier and
save wear and tear on the bit.

Standard wallboard is
4' x 8' and 1/2" thick.

Install planks for a deck bark side up.

When installing a tub,
put insulation underneath it.
It will reduce noise and
keep the water warmer for a
longer period of time.

For easier cleaning, use
semigloss on most doors and trim.
It's also a good choice to use on
bathroom and kitchen walls.

When painting a room,
paint the ceiling first.

Flat paint will hide many
imperfections on most walls
and ceilings.

Common nails are best for most
carpentry. Their broad heads will
not pull through wood.

Paint the exterior of your house in
the spring or the fall.

Use a guide when routering.

Do not shake a can of varnish
as it causes bubbles.

Put a light coat of wax on the
metal parts of your tools and oil on
the wood parts before putting
them away for the winter.

To prevent wood from splitting,
drive nails in a staggered pattern.

Use wood biscuits when joining wood end to end. They are invisible when the project is completed and add strength to joints.

Lower wattage light bulbs generally last longer.

For easy removal of concrete forms,
coat them with oil before pouring
the concrete.

When applying polyurethane,
work from the center of the project
to the outside.

Store cement mix in a dry place on
a raised platform.

Only hire a licensed contractor.

Replace air conditioner and furnace
filters once a month.

An electrical circuit is a continuous path of electricity starting from the power source to the power-using appliance and then back to the power source. When an appliance is turned off, power does not flow.

To get optimal performance from
your hot water heater, drain the
tank once every six months.

Use surge protectors for
your power tools, computers, and
other electrical appliances.

Never replace
a fuse with one of
higher amperage.

Always unplug
an appliance before
you repair it.

Pull a cord from
an outlet at the plug,
never by the cord.

Do not run an extension
cord under a rug or where it could
cause someone to trip.

Tie a knot between the
ends of two electrical cords before
plugging them together.

Use spring metal key rings or locks
in the prongs of power tool cords to
prevent children from using them.

To allow for expansion, use
a nickel to space the proper width
between wood paneling.

To increase holding power,
put adhesive on studs before
sheetrocking.

When installing floor tile start in the center of the room and work toward the walls.

Central heat and air conditioning systems should be serviced twice a year, in the fall and spring.

When you are stumped during
a project, save time by consulting
a book or an expert, instead of
repeated trial and error.

Always use a push stick when
working with a table saw.

Have a well-lit, well-ventilated work area.

Never point a paint gun at
yourself or another person.

Keep ladders away from overhead
electrical lines.

Use tools only for their
intended purposes.

Put a smoke alarm in every room.

It's not always best to buy
all new materials.

To keep track of loose
screws, tape them to the object
to which they belong.

When patching a hole
in drywall, enlarge the hole to
a regular shape.

When using a ladder, place it so the distance between the wall and the bottom of the ladder is about one quarter the heighth of the ladder.

Put charcoal, chalk, or mothballs in a tool box to absorb moisture.

When insulating, ceilings should generally have an R-value between 26 and 38, and walls should generally have an R-value between 11 and 17.

Texturing a ceiling covers many irregularities.

Fifteen to fifty percent of energy costs in older buildings are due to air leaks. Caulk and weather stripping can bring the biggest savings in battling heat loss.

Use fiberglass insulation to cover
the exterior surfaces of air and
heat ducts in the attic.

Use a paint guard
when cutting in. It's a lot faster
than using masking tape.

The rise is the
vertical height of a stairway
from floor to floor.

The run is the
horizontal length of
a stairway.

When possible, do the
work yourself. You can save
a lot of money.

Cleaning your refrigerator
condenser plates will prolong
the life of the appliance.

Termites can be present
without visible signs. Have
regular inspections.

Store flammables
such as paints and solvents in
a locked metal cabinet.

To save money,
lower your hot water heater
temperature.

Weather-stripping and
acoustical tile on doors will reduce
noise from the workshop to the
rest of the house.

Do not remove your table
saw blade guard.

To carry sheets of plywood by yourself, hook a loop of rope around the
bottom corners of the wood
and pick up the center of the rope.

Unplug your tools when they are
not being used.

Cap outlets in your workshop to prevent sawdust from getting in them and creating a fire hazard.

Store clean rags in a cut plastic jug and hang it from your pegboard.

When storing items, glue or tape
a sample of the item to the outside
of the storage container for quick
and easy identification.

Scrap plywood can be used to make
small storage boxes.

For extra storage space,
build shelves on the underside
of a stairway.

Coat the blade of a
steel tape measure with paste wax
to prevent rusting.

To prevent hitting your
thumb or fingers with a
hammer, push a nail through
a piece of cardboard and hold
it by the edge away from the
nail when hammering.

Other ways to prevent hitting your
thumb or finger with a hammer:
hold a nail with an old comb,
tweezers, or a bobby pin.

Keep a spare, charged battery
for your cordless tools.

A nail hammered through a hole in a scrap of pegboard will prevent damage to the surface you are hammering on.

To pull headless nails lever the hammer sideways.

Old tennis balls cut with slits can be used to protect the heads of wood chisels during storage.

To magnetize a screwdriver, pull a magnet down the length of the shaft four or five times.

An easy and accurate way to mark an outlet box when installing sheets of plywood or sheet rock: mark carpenter's chalk on the outside edges of the box and press the board against it. The chalk will make an outline showing where to cut.

Put a lock through the hole of your saw trigger to prevent unwanted use.

When gluing an object using clamps, put wax paper between the clamps and the object to prevent them from sticking together.

When cutting on a sawhorse, one method of holding a board steady is to slide an old bicycle inner tube over the board and use your foot to stretch the tube taut to the floor.

Vacuum the motor housings of
your power tools.

Store glue bottles upside down.

Choose latex based glues over
solvent glues for easier cleanup.

For contour sanding, wrap
sandpaper around a deck of cards.

A trash bag taped to the
bottom of your table saw will collect
a good deal of sawdust and
save on cleanup time.

Use a drinking straw or a cotton swab to remove excess glue from the inside corners of a project.

You can make a quick apron by cutting holes in a plastic bag for your head and arms.

Taping a penlight to your drill can add an extra spotlight for your work.

To determine where to place hooks for a wall hanging, tape a paper cutout of similar size to your wall and then make marks behind the cutout.

A handy place to keep bee's wax:
drill a small hole in the
bottom of a hammer and
fill it with bee's wax.

To clean grease off your hands, try
rubbing them in sawdust.

Turn an old paintbrush into a dustbrush by cutting the stiff portion of the bristles off.

Keep items from rolling off your stepladder platform by attaching molding around the edges.

Drill a hole in a curved
surface by center punching the
spot on which you will drill.
Then cover the spot with a piece
of masking tape and drill
through the tape.

Tape a piece of medium grade
sandpaper to your workbench
for quick and handy sharpening
of shop pencils.

Emery boards can be used for
sanding small projects.

Stick magnetized rubber
strips on your vise to protect
wood surfaces.

Plug a night light into the end of an
extension cord to shed light into an
area where a floodlight will not fit.

Secure a rubber band around the handles of a pair of pliers to hold it snugly around an object.

When cutting glass, brush paint thinner along the cutting line to reduce friction.

If the edge of your
chisel blade is shiny it needs
to be sharpened.

Put a piece of panty hose
over the filter of your shop vacuum
to prolong its life.

**Nail a yardstick
to the top of your sawhorse for
quick measuring.**

**Mark volume measurements
on the inside of a bucket to make
measuring easier.**

Sketch projects on
graph paper to determine
proper proportions.

Use diluted bleach to
remove mildew from the
exterior of your house.

When using a ladder, hold
items in a small basket placed
on the ladder shelf.

To make small pilot holes,
use a finishing nail rather than an
expensive drill bit.

To clean a paintbrush effectively
after using latex paint,
brush off excess paint, then rinse
with warm soapy water while
spreading and squeezing the paint
out of the bristles.

Take vitamin C after
being exposed to paint fumes.
It is an antitoxin.

Fill nail holes *after* you
stain or varnish so the wood putty
does not absorb the stain.

Varnish will adhere
better if you thin it with
mineral spirits.

Putting trim nails along the
lines of the grain will help hide
them naturally.

Adding a little food coloring to wallpaper paste will make it easier to
see. Just a little tint is sufficient.

Remove old wallpaper paste
by spraying walls with warm water
and using a squeegee.

You can use a paint roller as a substitute for a wallpaper brush.

To make a better match when patching wallpaper tear the patch instead of cutting.
The ragged edges blend in better.

Spray a disinfectant on the paste
side of wallpaper before you put it on
the wall to help prevent mildewing.

Mix white vinegar in with
plaster to keep it wet longer while
you are working with it.

To prevent warping when paneling, attach wallboard to studs and then glue the paneling to the wallboard.

Corn starch mixed with water is a good glass cleaner.

To remove a piece of vinyl tile
put a piece of cloth on top of it and
run a hot iron over it.

To open a painted-shut window,
try running a utility knife in
the groove that was painted.

Petroleum jelly in your
window tracks will facilitate
opening and closing.

Use graphite or silicone to
lubricate tracks for sliding doors.
They attract less dirt than oils.

To prevent fingerprints, wear gloves
when glazing windows.

Put a swollen drawer in the
hot sun. After it dries out, coat
it with a wood preservative to
prevent further swelling.

Tap a screw with a hammer a few times before the last couple of twists. It will have a better bite in the wood.

To prevent splitting a thin piece of wood, dull the nail head before driving.

To put a screw into an oversized hole, first stick toothpicks coated with glue in the hole and let dry.

To prevent splintering while sawing plywood, put a strip of masking tape over the cutting line.

To prevent your circular saw from
jamming when cutting sheets
of plywood, try putting an
extra piece of scrap wood
behind the saw (in the kerf of
the cut) to keep the pieces apart.

To keep a saw from sliding when cutting metal, make a notch in the metal with a file and then cut.

Attach a washer to a nut with rubber cement. It will then be easier to screw them onto a bolt.

To start a nail in a hard-to-reach
place, first wedge the nail
into the claw of a hammer and
punch it into the wood,
then hammer it in.

Use a hammer drill for concrete.

A few strands of steel wool placed
on the gluing surface of a wood joint
will add strength to the bond.

An auto hose clamp can
be used to clamp round pieces of
broken wood while gluing.

You can remove a ding from a wood
surface with an iron and a wet cloth.

To sand a small piece of wood,
rub it against the sandpaper
rather than rubbing the sandpaper
against the wood.

Contact paper on the back of sandpaper will prevent it from tearing when
it is on your sander or sanding block.

Attach a sheet of sandpaper
to a block of wood to make your
own block sander.

Hydrogen peroxide is a good
substitute for penetrating oil.

Put weather stripping around
your attic hatch and insulation
on top of it to eliminate a
large source of heat loss.

Use mineral oil when
lubricating kitchen appliances.
It's nontoxic.

Rub rotting wood with a wire
brush and then apply salt to get
rid of rot-causing fungus.

A vent in closet doors will help
deter must and mildew.

To remove a grease stain from
concrete, spread mineral spirits
and whiting over the stain. Let the
mixture dry, then brush it off.

For a grease clog in the trap of a sink, try warming the outside of the pipe with a hand-held dryer and then run very hot water into the pipe.

White vinegar rubbed on counters and floors will help keep ants away.

Scrub mildewed wood with
diluted bleach and then coat
with wood sealer.

In a pinch, a straightened-out coat
hanger can serve as a replacement
for a plumber's snake.

An auto hose clamp can be used to tighten a loose plunger handle.

Coat the threads of a drain pipe with petroleum jelly. The pipes will be easier to work with the next time repairs are needed.

Wire spare washers to pipes under sinks to save time during future drain repairs.

Tie a wrench that fits the cutoff valve to your gas line. It will save time in case of an emergency.

A plastic straw over the
lift chain in your toilet tank will
prevent the chain from getting
caught in the flapper valve.

Outside awnings over windows and
doors will keep rooms cooler.

Plastic containers filled
with water and placed in the toilet
tank will decrease the amount
of water needed to refill the
tank, thereby conserving water
and saving money.

An electronic ignition on your
water heater will prove cheaper
in the long run and is
also safer than a gas pilot.

For better efficiency, keep air
conditioners out of direct sunlight.

Cover attic fan louvers in the winter to avoid heat loss.

When heating oil is delivered, shut down the furnace for half an hour after delivery to allow sediment to settle.

To increase the life-span of
a light bulb or battery,
try cleaning the terminal with
a pencil eraser.

Clean radiator baseboards three
times a year.

Hang this book
on your workbench from a
hook or peg.

Use the following
pages of graph paper to
sketch projects.